Vultures/Buitres

By JoAnn Early Macken

Reading Consultant: Jeanne Clidas, Ph.D.
Director, Roberts Wesleyan College Literacy Clinic

WEEKLY READER®
PUBLISHING

Please visit our web site at **www.garethstevens.com**.
For a free catalog describing our list of high-quality books,
call 1-877-542-2595 (USA) or 1-800-387-3178 (Canada).
Our fax: 1-877-542-2596

Library of Congress Cataloging-in-Publication Data

Macken, JoAnn Early, 1953–
    [Vultures. Spanish & English]
    Vultures = Buitres / by JoAnn Early Macken; reading consultant, Jeanne Clidas.
        p. cm. — (Animals that live in the desert = Animales del desierto)
    Includes bibliographical references and index.
    English and Spanish; translated from the English.
    ISBN-10: 1-4339-2424-2   ISBN-13: 978-1-4339-2424-8 (lib. bdg.)
    ISBN-10: 1-4339-2461-7   ISBN-13: 978-1-4339-2461-3 (soft cover)
    1. Vultures—Juvenile literature. I. Title. II. Title: Buitres.
  QL696.F32M257318   2010
  598.9'2—dc22
                                                 2009009784

This edition first published in 2010 by
Weekly Reader® Books
An Imprint of Gareth Stevens Publishing
1 Reader's Digest Road
Pleasantville, NY 10570-7000 USA

Copyright © 2010 by Gareth Stevens, Inc.

Executive Managing Editor: Lisa M. Herrington
Senior Editor: Barbara Bakowski
Cover Designers: Jennifer Ryder-Talbot and Studio Montage
Production: Studio Montage
Translators: Tatiana Acosta and Guillermo Gutiérrez
Library Consultant: Carl Harvey, Library Media Specialist, Noblesville, Indiana

Photo credits: Cover, pp. 1, 5, 9, 19 Shutterstock; pp. 7, 15, 17 © Richard Day/Daybreak Imagery;
p. 11 © Elio Della Ferrera/naturepl.com; p. 13 © Lynn M. Stone; p. 21 © Todd Fink/Daybreak Imagery

Printed in the United States of America

1 2 3 4 5 6 7 8 9 14 13 12 11 10 09

Table of Contents

- - - - - - - - - - - - - - - - -

Contenido

Boldface words appear in the glossary./
Las palabras en **negrita** aparecen en el glosario.

Meat Eaters

Vultures are large birds with long wings. They are **raptors**. Raptors are birds that eat meat. Some vultures live in the **desert**.

- - - - - - - - - - - - - - -

Aves que comen carne

Los buitres son aves grandes con largas alas. Son **aves rapaces**. Las aves rapaces comen carne. Algunos buitres viven en el **desierto**.

Vultures fly high in circles. They soar for a long time without flapping their wings. While they fly, they look for food.

- - - - - - - - - - - - -

Los buitres vuelan en círculo a gran altura. Pueden planear durante mucho tiempo sin batir las alas. Mientras vuelan, los buitres buscan comida.

Vultures do not have to kill their food.
They eat dead animals. They can smell
a dead animal from far away. They swoop
in to eat it.

- - - - - - - - - - - - - - -

Los buitres no tienen que matar a los
animales que se comen. Se alimentan de
animales muertos. Los buitres pueden oler
un animal muerto a mucha distancia. Se
abalanzan sobre él para comérselo.

Vultures also look for sick animals. When a sick animal dies, the vultures eat it. Dead animals are called **carrion**.

- - - - - - - - - - - - - -

Los buitres también buscan animales enfermos. Cuando un animal enfermo muere, los buitres se lo comen. Los restos de los animales muertos se llaman **carroña**.

carrion/
carroña

Ready to Eat

Vultures have hooked **beaks**. Their hooked beaks help them tear meat apart.

- - - - - - - - - - - - - -

Listos para comer

Los buitres tienen el **pico** ganchudo. La forma del pico los ayuda a desgarrar la carne.

beak/
pico

Vultures have long, thin necks. They have few feathers on their heads. Their heads stay clean when they eat.

- - - - - - - - - - - - - - -

Los buitres tienen el cuello largo y delgado. Tienen pocas plumas en la cabeza. Así no se ensucian la cabeza cuando comen.

Starting a Family

Some vultures build nests out of sticks. Some vultures do not build nests. They hide their eggs on the ground or in trees.

- - - - - - - - - - - - - -

Empezar una familia

Algunos buitres usan palos para hacer nidos. Otros buitres no hacen nidos. Esconden sus huevos en el suelo o en árboles.

eggs/
huevos

17

Baby vultures hatch from the eggs. They are called **chicks**. The chicks are covered with **down**.

- - - - - - - - - - - - - -

De los huevos, salen las crías de los buitres. Las crías, o **polluelos**, están cubiertas de **plumón**.

18

chick/
polluelo

down/
plumón

Their parents keep the chicks warm.
Their parents feed them meat until they
can hunt on their own.

- - - - - - - - - - - - - - -

Los padres dan calor a los polluelos.
Los alimentan con carne hasta que los
polluelos pueden cazar solos.

Fast Facts/Datos básicos

Height/ Altura	about 2 feet (61 centimeters)/ unos 2 pies (61 centímetros)
Wingspan/ Envergadura	about 6 feet (2 meters)/ unos 6 pies (2 metros)
Weight/ Peso	about 10 pounds (5 kilograms)/ unas 10 libras (5 kilogramos)
Diet/ Dieta	mostly dead animals/ sobre todo animales muertos
Average life span/ Promedio de vida	up to 24 years/ hasta 24 años

Glossary/Glosario

beaks: the bills of birds

carrion: the flesh of dead animals

chicks: baby birds

desert: a dry area with little rainfall

down: soft, fluffy feathers

raptors: birds that eat meat

- - - - - - - - - - - - - - - - - -

aves rapaces: aves que comen carne

carroña: carne de los animales muertos

desierto: zona seca donde cae poca lluvia

pico: parte de la cabeza de las aves

plumón: plumas suaves y esponjosas

polluelos: crías de aves

For More Information/Más información

Books/Libros

Vultures. Ugly Animals (series). Kerri O'Donnell
(Powerkids Press, 2006)

What Desert Animals Eat/¿Qué comen los animales del desierto?
Nature's Food Chains (series). Joanne Mattern
(Gareth Stevens, 2006)

Web Sites/Páginas web

Turkey Vulture/Buitre americano
www.birds.cornell.edu/AllAboutBirds/BirdGuide/
Turkey_Vulture.html
Hear a hissing vulture and learn cool facts./Oigan el silbido
de un buitre y aprendan datos fascinantes.

Turkey Vulture/Buitre americano
www.natureali.org/TVfacts.htm
This site features many interesting facts and great photos./
Esta página web contiene muchos datos interesantes y
excelentes fotografías.

Index/Índice

About the Author

JoAnn Early Macken is the author of two rhyming picture books, *Sing-Along Song* and *Cats on Judy*, and more than 80 nonfiction books for children. Her poems have appeared in several children's magazines. She lives in Wisconsin with her husband and their two sons.

Información sobre la autora

JoAnn Early Macken ha escrito dos libros de rimas con ilustraciones, *Sing-Along Song* y *Cats on Judy*, y más de ochenta libros de no ficción para niños. Sus poemas han sido publicados en varias revistas infantiles. Vive en Wisconsin con su esposo y sus dos hijos.

24